THE OFFICIAL
CHELSEA FC
ANNUAL 2017

Written by David Antill, Richard Godden,
James Sugrue and Dominic Bliss
Designed by Chris Dalrymple
Thanks to Kevin Newman and Sarah Cobb

A Grange Publication

©2016. Published by Grange Communications Ltd., Edinburgh, under licence from
Chelsea FC Merchandising Limited. www.chelseafc.com. Printed in the EU.

ISBN: 978-1-911287-03-2

CONTENTS

The passion of opening day is palpable as the players make their way onto the pitch at Stamford Bridge for the first game of the season against West Ham.

WELCOME

Welcome, Chelsea fans, to The Official Chelsea FC Annual 2017!

We have got lots in the coming pages to keep you entertained, including games, stats, great pics and chats with your favourite Blues.

There's your chance to find out everything about the boss, Antonio Conte, the latest Italian legend to come to Stamford Bridge, as well as a special tribute to JT and profiles of every player in the squad for this season.

You can catch up on the Academy's achievements and the youngsters looking to break into the first team, as well as all the action from the wonderful Chelsea Ladies team. Then Stamford has all the laughs from behind the scenes and much, much more.

So delve inside, get your Chelsea fix and remember to keep the blue flag flying high!

EVERYTHING YOU NEED TO KNOW ABOUT ANTONIO CONTE!

We give you the low down on the Chelsea boss...

CHAMPION PLAYER

As a player Antonio Conte was an energetic central midfielder, who never stopped running. He ran from box-to-box with power and determination, passed well, all the while creating and scoring his fair share of goals. He spent most of his career with Juventus after moving there from his home-town club Lecce in 1991. In 12 years with 'Juve', Conte was a key player in one of the most successful sides of the 1990s, and was even named captain due to his influence over the squad and the example he set with his great attitude.

He was also a serial winner. Over the course of 13 years with Juventus, Conte won five league titles, as well as the Champions League, the UEFA Cup, the UEFA Super Cup, the Intercontinental Cup and the Italian Cup. Overall, he played 418 games for the club and scored 43 goals.

A NATURAL COACH

Conte retired from playing in 2004 and it wasn't long before he decided to become a coach. After starting out with Arezzo, he achieved success in his second role as a manager when he won promotion to Italy's top division, Serie A, with Bari. His next job was with top-flight Atalanta, and then he moved to Siena, who he also led to promotion to Serie A.

With two promotions to his name, Conte was viewed as one of the most promising managers in Italy and, in 2011, his old club Juventus named him as their new boss.

In the season before Conte arrived back at the club, Juventus had finished seventh in the league, but he immediately turned them into champions, winning the league in his first season in charge. Even more incredibly, his team didn't lose a single game on their way to taking the Serie A title.

He went on to win the league the next two seasons as well, making it three titles in a row for Conte's Juventus between 2012 and 2014. The third title was won with a record points total of 102 – the first time in history any Italian team had achieved more than 100 points.

At the end of three amazing years with the club from Turin, Conte was asked to become the new manager of Italy in 2014, and he left Juventus as a hero.

INTERNATIONAL HERO

During his playing days, Conte won 20 international caps for Italy, scoring twice. He was part of the squad as the 'Azzurri' reached the World Cup final in 1994 and also the final of Euro 2000.

Fourteen years later, he returned to the national team ... this time as coach. He led his country to Euro 2016 without losing a single qualifying game and then proceeded to win a tough group, after beating Belgium and Sweden in their opening two matches last summer. His team then went on to knock out reigning champions Spain before losing out to Germany in the quarter-finals on sudden death penalty kicks. Many announced that Conte had led the team brilliantly, showcasing his masterful tactical and motivational skills and uniting the players behind the cause.

A NEW ERA

After arriving at Chelsea in the summer, Conte quickly revealed how he likes to do things and what he aims to achieve during his time at Stamford Bridge.

"I'm excited for this moment and to start a new season with Chelsea," he said. "It's a new chapter in my life, for my career, for me and for my family. I'm very happy to start working in a fantastic country and fantastic league.

"I am a worker. I like to work. I know only this road to win, to get this club competing very soon, to play in the Champions League, to win the title. I know only this verb – work, work, work.

"Usually, if you have great organisation and the great talent of the players and you also run more than the others, then you have more probability of winning. For this reason I like to work on all aspects: tactical, technical, physical and mental.

"This is the right challenge and I'm sure with the players and the club all together we can achieve great satisfaction at the end of the season."

AZZURRI BLUES

Chelsea and Italy both play in blue and, in fact, the Italian national team's nickname, 'Gli Azzurri' means 'The Blues' when translated into English.
So it seems only right that we have such a strong historical connection to Italy. After all, Antonio Conte has joined a long line of Italian legends to represent Chelsea. Let's take a look back at some of the fans' favourites:

Gianfranco Zola

He arrived in November 1996 from Parma and ended his first season in England as the Football Writers' Footballer of the Year, as Chelsea won the FA Cup. Gianfranco Zola is only 5ft 5in but his wonderful skill, his mesmerising dribbling and his curling shots from the edge of the area made him a joy to watch. Over the course of seven seasons at Stamford Bridge, he became one of the most loved players in the club's history, scoring 80 goals in 312 games.

Gianluca Vialli

When he joined Chelsea in the summer of 1996, Gianluca Vialli was one of the most famous footballers in the world. The bald striker was part of an exciting period at the club, as we went from strength to strength in the late 1990s and, when Ruud Gullit's reign in the dugout came to an end in February 1998, Vialli became Chelsea manager. He won the FA Cup, the League Cup, the European Cup Winners' Cup, the UEFA Super Cup and the Charity Shield as Blues boss, having already won the FA Cup as a player. He also led us into the Champions League for the first time in our history in 1999/2000, reaching the quarter-final stage.

Roberto Di Matteo

Another star who joined Chelsea in 1996, Roberto Di Matteo turned out to be a cup final specialist, both as player and manager. As a box-to-box midfielder he scored in the 1997 and 2000 FA Cup Finals, as well as the 1998 League Cup Final, all of which Chelsea won. Then, as manager, he led the club to Champions League and FA Cup glory in 2012.

Carlo Cudicini

Despite arriving as a back-up goalkeeper in 1999, Carlo Cudicini's performances when called into the team were so impressive that he soon became first-choice and is considered to be one of the best keepers in Chelsea's history. In total, Cudicini played 216 times for Chelsea in 10 years at Stamford Bridge, winning the club's Player of the Year award in 2002. He is now an official club ambassador.

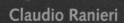

Carlo Ancelotti

Considering he won the Premier League and FA Cup Double in his first season as Chelsea manager, it's fair to say Carlo Ancelotti got off to a good start at Stamford Bridge. His 2009/10 champions broke the league record for the number of goals scored in a single season, with 103, making them the first team to score more than 100 goals in a Premier League campaign.

Claudio Ranieri

You may know him as the manager who won the Premier League with Leicester City last season, but for four years between 2000 and 2004 Claudio Ranieri was Chelsea boss. It was a different time for the club, when we were not as strong as we have been over the last decade or so, but in his time here Ranieri steered Chelsea back to a Champions League qualifying position in 2003 and reached the semi-finals the following season, as well as finishing second in the Premier League.

JOHN TERRY 70

The 2015/16 season saw John Terry become only the third player to reach 700 Chelsea appearances. We all know the Blues skipper is a world-class defender, but it's the length of time that JT has been at the top of his game for that is really amazing.

It was last century when he made his first-team debut at the age of 18, in a League Cup fixture against Aston Villa, way back in October 1998. But his link with Chelsea goes back even further than that. He joined the club when he was just 14 and, after signing a new one-year contract with us in the summer, he has extended his time with the Blues to an incredible 22 years.

In the modern era, there aren't many players who can claim to have shown such loyalty to one club, which is why JT will always be our Captain, Leader, Legend.

Over the next four pages you can look back at the career of JT and find out some fascinating facts about him you can tell all your mates.

JT was an unused substitute in the final when he won his first major honour with Chelsea, the 2000 FA Cup. He had scored his first senior goal for the club in our quarter-final win over Gillingham.

Posing with the Chelsea Player of the Year award in 2001. He also won it in 2006.

This is JT at our old training ground in 2002. How many times have you seen him rise like this to head the ball clear in a game? As they say, practice makes perfect.

The early years:
Season 1999/2000.

JT was named captain full-time at the start of the 2004/05 season and at the end of that campaign he was celebrating being a Premier League winner for the first time.

JOHN TERRY 700

Although he was suspended for the final, JT played a key role as we won the Champions League for the first time in 2012. He is pictured here with Roman Abramovich after our memorable win over Bayern Munich.

JT revealed a special T-shirt when he made his 500th appearance as Chelsea captain, in a 2-1 win over Crystal Palace in 2014.

Celebrating our most recent Premier League triumph in 2015. JT played every minute of every league game that season and was named in the PFA Team of the Year.

Scoring the first goal at Wembley in our 2-0 win over Tottenham in the 2015 Capital One Cup final.

In 2010, he led the club to our first-ever FA Cup and Premier League Double.

Celebrating one of his most famous goals for the club – when we beat Barcelona in the Champions League in 2005. No defender has scored more goals for Chelsea than JT. He had found the back of the net 66 times by the end of last season and is also the highest-scoring defender in Premier League history.

JT showed he's a pretty good goalie when he went between the sticks in a game against Reading in 2006 after Petr Cech and Carlo Cudicini were injured. He kept a clean sheet in a 1-0 win.

PLAYER PROFILES

Here are the players looking to lead the Blues to glory in the 2016/17 season.

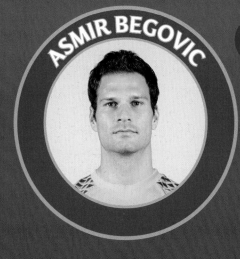

Position: Goalkeeper **Height:** 6ft 6in **Born:** Trebinje, Bosnia and Herzegovina, 20.06.1987 **Signed from:** Stoke City (July 2015) **Chelsea appearances:** 25 **Clean sheets:** 8

Did you know? Asmir's wife Nicolle partakes in dressage, which is widely recognised as the sport of the dancing horses!

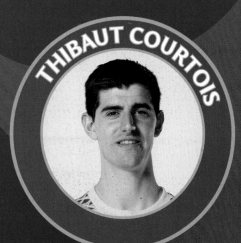

Position: Goalkeeper **Height:** 6ft 6in **Born:** Bree, Belgium, 11.05.1992 **Signed from:** Genk (July 2011) **Chelsea appearances:** 69 **Clean sheets:** 22

Did you know? The keeper strayed from his family's sporting path, as both of his parents and his sister have been professional volleyball players.

Position: Goalkeeper **Height:** 6ft 2in **Born:** Mirandela, Portugual, 19.09.1982 **Signed from:** Dinamo Zagreb (August 2016) **Chelsea appearances:** 0 **Clean sheets:** 0

Did you know? Eduardo was a team-mate of Diego Costa when the pair played for Portuguese side Braga.

Position: Defender **Height:** 5ft 10in **Born:** Pamplona, Spain, 28.08.1989 **Signed from:** Marseille (August 2012) **Chelsea appearances:** 181 **Goals:** 3

Did you know? Like Didier Drogba and Michy Batshuayi, Azpi joined the Blues from Marseille.

FIKAYO TOMORI

Position: Defender **Height:** 6ft 1in **Born:** Calgary, Canada, 19.12.1997 **Turned pro:** July 2015 **Chelsea appearances:** 1 **Goals:** 0

Did you know? Fikayo scored in the final of both the FA Youth Cup and UEFA Youth League in 2016.

BRANISLAV IVANOVIC

Position: Defender **Height:** 6ft 1in **Born:** Sremska Mitrovica, Serbia, 22.02.1984 **Signed from:** Lokomotiv Moscow (January 2008) **Chelsea appearances:** 361 **Goals:** 33

Did you know? As well as acting as Chelsea's vice-captain, Branner wears the armband for his country.

OLA AINA

Position: Defender **Height:** 6ft **Born:** London, England, 08.10.1996 **Turned pro:** October 2013 **Chelsea appearances:** 0 **Goals:** 0

Did you know? Ola appeared in 20 consecutive FA Youth Cup matches, spread across three seasons.

JOHN TERRY

Position: Defender **Height:** 6ft 2in **Born:** London, England, 07.12.1980 **Turned pro:** March 1998 **Chelsea appearances:** 703 **Goals:** 66

Did you know? This is the 19th season of John Terry's remarkable career in the Chelsea first team.

KURT ZOUMA

Position: Defender **Height:** 6ft 3in **Born:** Lyon, France, 27.10.1994 **Signed from:** Saint-Etienne (January 2014) **Chelsea appearances:** 58 **Goals:** 4

Did you know? Kurt's father named him after Jean Claude Van Damme's character in the 1989 film *Kickboxer* and his middle name is Happy!

GARY CAHILL

Position: Defender Height: 6ft 4in Born: Sheffield, England, 19.12.1985 Signed from: Bolton Wanderers (January 2012) Chelsea appearances: 196 Goals: 17

Did you know? Gaz had only spent three and a half years with Chelsea when he completed a full set of major honours!

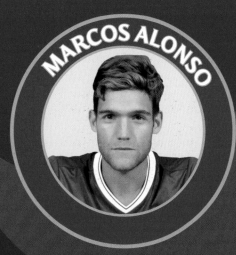

MARCOS ALONSO

Position: Defender Height: 6ft 2in
Born: Madrid, Spain, 28.12.1990 Signed from: Fiorentina (August 2016) Chelsea appearances: 0 Goals: 0

Did you know? This is Marcos's third spell in the Premier League as he has previously played for Bolton Wanderers and Sunderland.

DAVID LUIZ

Position: Defender Height: 6ft 2in
Born: Diadema, Brazil, 22.04.1987 Signed from: Paris Saint-Germain (August 2016) Chelsea appearances: 143 Clean sheets: 12

Did you know? David Luiz was named in the FIFA World Team of the Year in 2014!

N'GOLO KANTÉ

Position: Midfielder Height: 5ft 7in Born: Paris, France, 29.03.91 Signed from: Leicester City (July 2016) Chelsea appearances: 0 Goals: 0

Did you know? N'Golo made 31 more tackles and 15 more interceptions than any other player in the 2015/16 Premier League season.

MARCO VAN GINKEL

Position: Midfielder Height: 6ft 1in
Born: Amersfoort, Netherlands, 01.12.1992 Signed from: Vitesse Arnhem (July 2013) Chelsea appearances: 4 Goals: 0

Did you know? Marco scored eight times to help PSV Eindhoven win the Eredivisie title in 2016.

CESC FÀBREGAS

Position: Midfielder Height: 5ft 11in Born: Arenys de Mar, Spain, 04.05.1987 Signed from: Barcelona (June 2014) Chelsea appearances: 96 Goals: 11

Did you know? Cesc has enjoyed an incredible international career, with over 100 caps to his name and winners' medals at two Euros and one World Cup!

NATHANIEL CHALOBAH

Position: Midfielder Height: 6ft 1in
Born: Freetown, Sierra Leone, 12.12.1994 Turned pro: January 2012 Chelsea appearances: 0 Goals: 0

Did you know? His brother Trevoh is currently in the Chelsea Academy and helped the Blues win the UEFA Youth League and FA Youth Cup last season.

JOHN MIKEL OBI

Position: Midfielder Height: 6ft 2in Born: Jos, Nigeria, 22.04.1987 Signed from: Lyn Oslo (June 2006)
Chelsea appearances: 372 Goals: 6

Did you know? Obi is Chelsea's second-longest serving player in the current first-team squad with 10 years' service behind him.

EDEN HAZARD

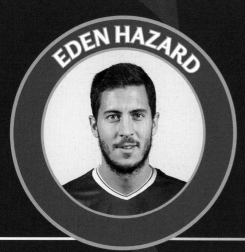

Position: Midfielder Height: 5ft 8in Born: La Louviere, Belgium, 07.01.1991 Signed from: Lille (June 2012) Chelsea appearances: 206 Goals: 55

Did you know? Only Antoine Griezmann was ahead of Eden in the joint rankings for goals and assists at Euro 2016.

RUBEN LOFTUS-CHEEK

Position: Midfielder Height: 6ft 3in Born: London, England, 23.01.1996 Turned pro: January 2013
Chelsea appearances: 21 Goals: 2

Did you know? Ruben has been with the club since Under-8s level, winning numerous major honours at youth level before stepping up to the first team in 2014.

PEDRO

Position: Midfielder Height: 5ft 6in Born: Santa Cruz de Tenerife, Spain, 28.07.1987 Signed from: Barcelona (August 2015) Chelsea appearances: 40 Goals: 8

Did you know? Pedro has won the Champions League three times in his career and was a scorer in the 2011 final against Man United.

NEMANJA MATIC

Position: Midfielder Height: 6ft 4in Born: Vrelo-Ub, Serbia, 01.08.1988 Signed from: Benfica (January 2014)
Chelsea appearances: 114 Goals: 5

Did you know? Three of Nemanja's appearances for the Blues came during a brief spell with the Blues earlier in his career.

WILLIAN

Position: Midfielder Height: 5ft 9in Born: Ribeirao Pires, Brazil, 09.08.1988 Signed from: Anzhi Makhachkala (August 2013)
Chelsea appearances: 140 Goals: 19

Did you know? The 2015/16 Player of the Year was lethal from free-kicks last season, scoring six of them before the end of November!

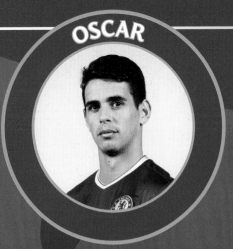

OSCAR

Position: Midfielder Height: 5ft 10in Born: Americana, Brazil, 09.09.1991 Signed from: Internacional (July 2012) Chelsea appearances: 192 Goals: 38

Did you know? Although he wasn't involved at Rio 2016, Oscar was part of the Brazil squad which won silver at the 2012 Olympics in London shortly before he joined the Blues.

VICTOR MOSES

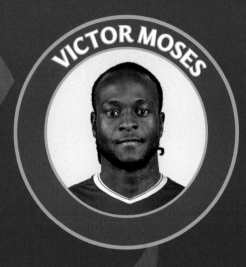

Position: Forward Height: 5ft 10in Born: Kaduna, Nigeria, 12.12.1990 Signed from: Wigan Athletic (August 2012) Chelsea appearances: 44 Goals: 10

Did you know? Victor was named Nigerian Footballer of the Year in 2013 after helping his country win the Africa Cup of Nations.

MICHY BATSHUAYI

Position: Forward Height: 6ft 1in Born: Brussels, Belgium, 02.10.1993 Signed from: Marseille (July 2016) Chelsea appearances: 0 Goals: 0

Did you know? Michy made an incredible debut at Euro 2016, scoring with his first touch of the tournament in Belgium's win over Hungary.

DIEGO COSTA

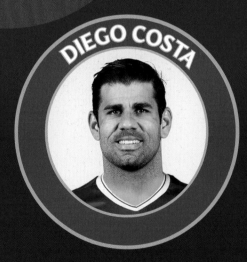

Position: Forward Height: 6ft 1in Born: Lagarto, Brazil, 07.10.1988 Signed from: Atletico Madrid (July 2014) Chelsea appearances: 78 Goals: 37

Did you know? Diego Costa has finished as Chelsea's top scorer in each of his two seasons at Stamford Bridge.

DOMINIC SOLANKE

Position: Forward Height: 6ft 2in Born: Reading, 14.09.1997 Turned pro: September 2014 Chelsea appearances: 1 Goals: 0

Did you know? Dominic was named England Men's Youth Player of the Year in 2014.

BLUES AROUND THE WORLD

Chelsea's first-team squad and coaching staff has been assembled from all corners of the globe. How much do you know about their home countries? Here is a selection of images linked to a few of these places, but can you assign the correct person to each picture?

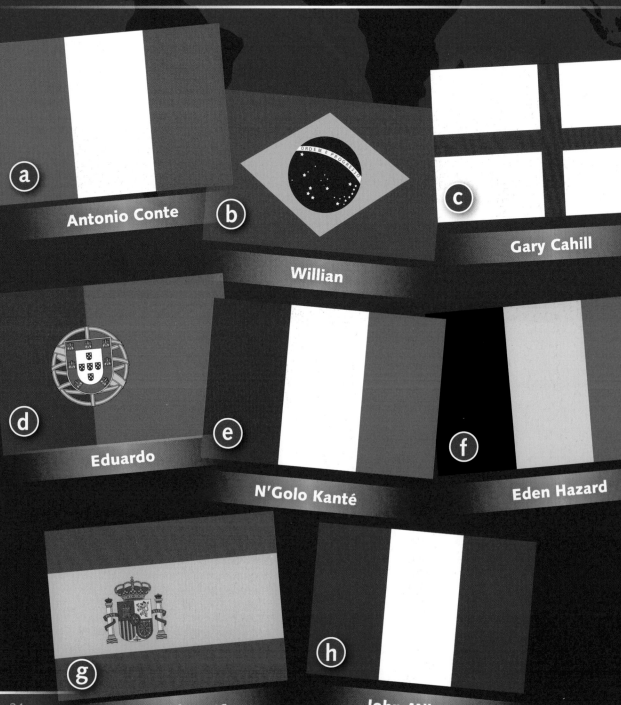

(a) **Antonio Conte**

(b) **Willian**

(c) **Gary Cahill**

(d) **Eduardo**

(e) **N'Golo Kanté**

(f) **Eden Hazard**

(g) **Cesc Fàbregas**

(h) **John Mikel Obi**

Answers on p61

1 Bullfighting is one of the traditional sports of this European country. Ole!

2 This country is the largest cork producer in the world - and plenty of those were popped after the European Championship...

3 Most of you probably love chocolate – but which country in Europe is famed for its production?

4 Christ the Redeemer is one of the major attractions that tourists flock to in this country, which also held the Olympics recently.

5 The world's most famous bike race takes place across this European country, which you can reach by train from England if you don't like flying!

6 This country won a bronze medal at Rio 2016 in the men's football tournament to go along with the gold they won in 1996.

7 Luciano Pavarotti was one of the world's most famous opera singers, but where in the world was this style of singing made popular?

8 There is only one place in the world where this is considered to be a culinary delight!

STADIUM TOUR
AND MUSEUM

KIDS' BIRTHDAY PARTIES
AT CHELSEA FC

Chelsea Stadium Tours & Museum offer a **unique** setting
for a truly **memorable** birthday...

FOR MORE INFORMATION
CALL 0371 811 1955 OR VISIT CHELSEAFC.COM/STADIUM-TOURS

Food is not included in the party, but can be arranged for an additional price.

GUESS WHO...

Can you work out who all four of these Chelsea players are?

- I joined from a Russian club
- I scored on my league debut against Norwich
- I played for Brazil at the 2014 World Cup

- I captained my country at Euro 2016
- I have been named Chelsea Player of the Year twice
- I scored the goal that won us the 2014/15 Premier League title

- I joined Chelsea in the summer of 2016
- I won the Premier League last season
- I was born in Paris

- I have played for Chelsea since 2008
- I wear the No2 shirt for the Blues
- I scored the winning goal in the 2013 Europa League final

Answers on p61

READ ALL ABOUT IT...

The matchday programme is a magazine that's been sold at Chelsea's home games since the club formed way back in 1905. Long before the internet and social media were invented, it was the only way fans could see pictures from our matches and read interviews with their favourite players.

The programme has changed massively over the years and here are some brilliant snippets, including some really old ones that even granny and granddad won't remember!

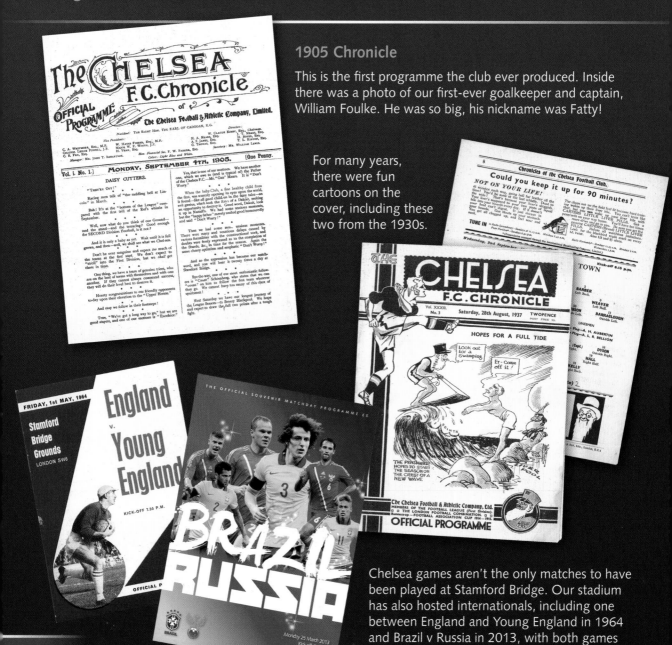

1905 Chronicle

This is the first programme the club ever produced. Inside there was a photo of our first-ever goalkeeper and captain, William Foulke. He was so big, his nickname was Fatty!

For many years, there were fun cartoons on the cover, including these two from the 1930s.

Chelsea games aren't the only matches to have been played at Stamford Bridge. Our stadium has also hosted internationals, including one between England and Young England in 1964 and Brazil v Russia in 2013, with both games featuring several Blues players.

In 1948, Chelsea created the first magazine-style programme. It was 16 pages and hugely popular – it sold out before the game had even kicked off!

1968-69 West Brom colour team shots

Programmes used to be completely black and white, but in the Sixties, colour photography gave things a whole new look.

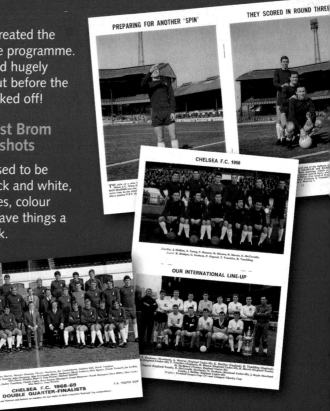

Since the 1990s, Chelsea have attracted the best players and managers in the world, and the programme has always had exclusive interviews and pictures with these legends.

UP FOR THE CUP!

Chelsea will celebrate the anniversary of two historic FA Cup triumphs in 2017. We take a look back at those memorable Wembley days out in 1997 and 2007...

1997 - BACK IN THE BIG TIME

The 1997 FA Cup final was one of the most memorable games in the history of Chelsea Football Club, not least because it was the first trophy we had won for 26 years!

Our opponents that day were Middlesbrough, who had already been relegated from the Premier League when they ran out to face an exciting Chelsea team at Wembley on a sunny afternoon in May.

Our manager was Ruud Gullit, who had once been one of the best players in the world and had become an instant hero when he joined Chelsea as a player in 1995. After winning the Supporters' Player of the Year award in his first season, he was named player-manager in the summer and his team played some of the best football Chelsea fans had seen for many years.

Gullit combined club legends like Dennis Wise, Eddie Newton and Steve Clarke with exciting foreign players with great talent, like Gianluca Vialli, Frank Leboeuf, Dan Petrescu and the wonderful Gianfranco Zola.

One of the most successful of all the new arrivals, though, was a midfielder called Roberto Di Matteo, and he was the man who made history in the 1997 FA Cup Final. His opening goal at Wembley that day came after just 43 seconds of the game! Middlesbrough didn't know what had hit them.

In the second half, Newton added a second goal from Zola's corner kick and Chelsea won the Cup. When the team brought the trophy back to west London on an open-top bus, supporters lined the streets in their tens of thousands to see it. Can you imagine what it meant to the supporters who had waited so long to see the Blues back at the top of the game?

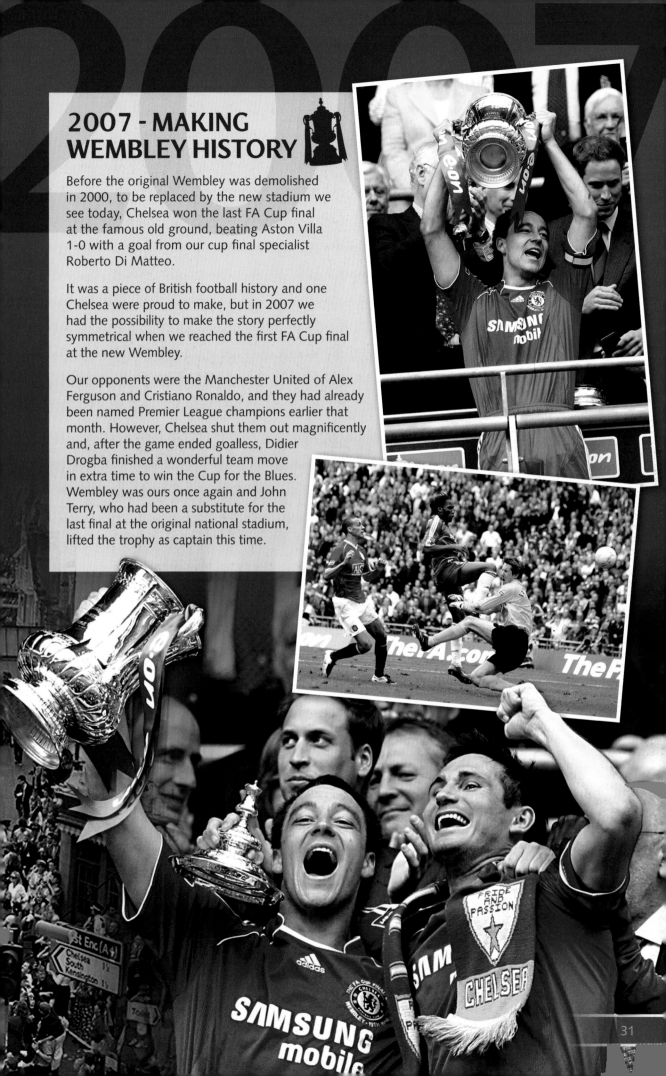

2007 - MAKING WEMBLEY HISTORY

Before the original Wembley was demolished in 2000, to be replaced by the new stadium we see today, Chelsea won the last FA Cup final at the famous old ground, beating Aston Villa 1-0 with a goal from our cup final specialist Roberto Di Matteo.

It was a piece of British football history and one Chelsea were proud to make, but in 2007 we had the possibility to make the story perfectly symmetrical when we reached the first FA Cup final at the new Wembley.

Our opponents were the Manchester United of Alex Ferguson and Cristiano Ronaldo, and they had already been named Premier League champions earlier that month. However, Chelsea shut them out magnificently and, after the game ended goalless, Didier Drogba finished a wonderful team move in extra time to win the Cup for the Blues. Wembley was ours once again and John Terry, who had been a substitute for the last final at the original national stadium, lifted the trophy as captain this time.

SKILL SET

These seven Chelsea stars tell you how they learned their silky skills and give you some advice on how to improve your own...

GARY CAHILL

How old were you when you first mastered keepy-uppies?

No idea! But I do remember something we did at school called the "Mars Bar challenge". You had to flick the ball from your foot to your knee to your shoulder to your head, and then on to your other shoulder, your other knee and your other foot. It was a big thing at school.

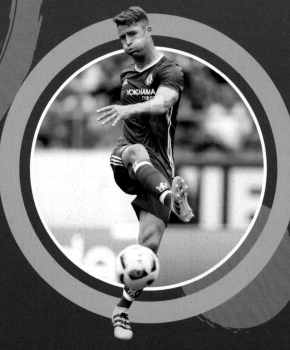

CESC FÀBREGAS

What skill do you think is underrated?

Using your first touch to dribble past an opponent. It's not really a dribble but you can use your touch and your body movement to go past somebody.

NEMANJA MATIC

At what age did you master keepy-uppies?

I was six. That's how I earned money for the first time. My dad promised me he would give me money to buy ice cream if I could reach 10, so that's what I did.

EDEN HAZARD

What particular skill did you work on most as a kid?

The nutmeg, which is known as panna in French, and also another skill which Zinedine Zidane used to do when he would spin on the ball. I still like the nutmeg, it's a good skill to use.

OSCAR

At what age did you first start kicking a ball around?

I can't remember exactly but very young. At five or six years I started to play football every day. I had a ball even younger, always practising, even inside the house as well as outside – all day, all the time!

WILLIAN

What is the best piece of skill you've produced in a game?

When I was playing for Brazil against Turkey I did the elastico and I did it against Argentina as well. For Chelsea I have also done some good skills but I can't pick one out.

DIEGO COSTA

What advice would you give to youngsters starting out in the game working on their skills?

Every child starting out has different abilities and they have their own skills and techniques. My advice would be to pick what you're best at and develop that, without losing your focus.

DOUBLE SUCCESS FOR BLUES YOUNGSTERS

EUROPEAN CROWN RETAINED

The UEFA Youth League is only three years old and Chelsea have already won it twice. Not bad, eh?

The competition is a Champions League for Under-19s teams and the semi-finals and the final are played over a four-day period in Nyon, the Swiss city where UEFA's headquarters are based.

After lifting the trophy in 2015, Chelsea's Under-19s returned to Switzerland for the finals weekend again at the end of last season, and after beating Belgian side Anderlecht 3-0 in the semi-finals, we faced a strong Paris Saint-Germain team.

No matter, Chelsea came out of the blocks flying and pressed the PSG players so well in the opening moments that they kept giving the ball away.

Fikayo Tomori gave Chelsea the lead from a Kasey Palmer corner, forcing home the rebound after fellow centre-back Jake Clarke-Salter's header had been blocked.

Bradley Collins then saved a penalty from PSG's Jean-Kevin Augustin but the French side eventually levelled 13 minutes into the second half. It served as a wake-up call for the Blues and they retook the lead three minutes later when Palmer scored a wonderful individual goal to decide the final and ensure that the trophy stays at Chelsea for another year.

THE FA YOUTH CUP

CHELSEA MAKE IT A YOUTH CUP HAT-TRICK

The Under-18s team celebrated silverware at the end of last season as well, as Chelsea became the first team since the 1950s to win the FA Youth Cup three times in a row! It was a fantastic achievement and we had to do it the hard way when we were pitted against Manchester City in the final for the second year running.

The first leg was played in Manchester and attacking midfielder Mason Mount gave Chelsea the lead with a great goal, although City equalised late in the game to leave the scores level ahead of the second leg at Stamford Bridge.

It was a thrilling night and when a thunder storm broke out in the middle of the game, the atmosphere really was electric! In the end, Chelsea were too strong for City and they ran out 3-1 winners on the night, making it 4-2 on aggregate, thanks to goals from Dujon Sterling, Tammy Abraham and Fikayo Tomori.

Chelsea's youth team were FA Youth Cup winners again and two of our players – captain Jake Clarke-Salter and left-back Jay Dasilva – won the famous old trophy for a record-equalling third time.

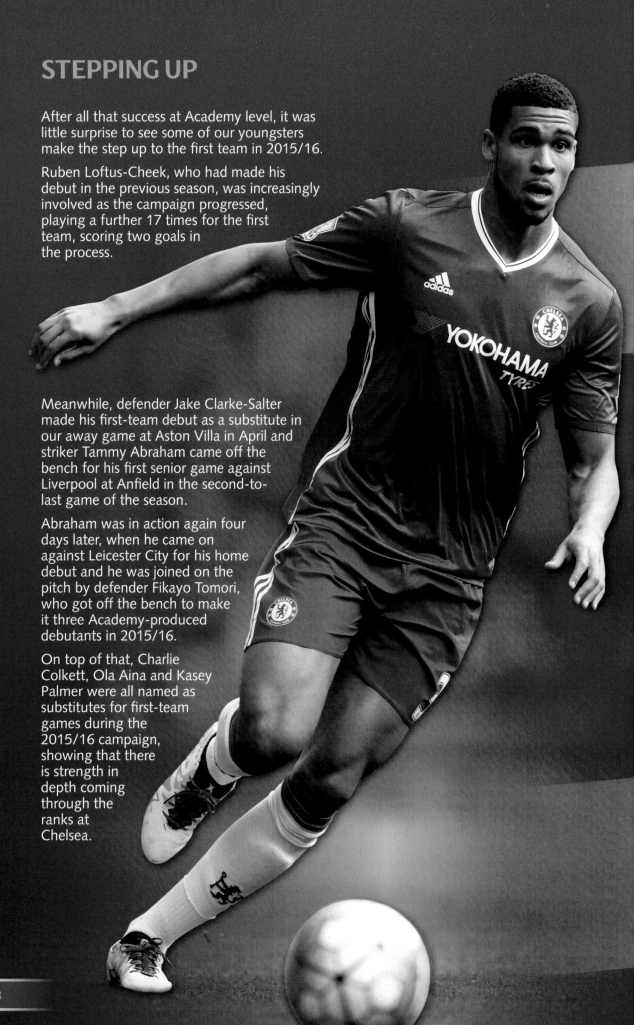

STEPPING UP

After all that success at Academy level, it was little surprise to see some of our youngsters make the step up to the first team in 2015/16.

Ruben Loftus-Cheek, who had made his debut in the previous season, was increasingly involved as the campaign progressed, playing a further 17 times for the first team, scoring two goals in the process.

Meanwhile, defender Jake Clarke-Salter made his first-team debut as a substitute in our away game at Aston Villa in April and striker Tammy Abraham came off the bench for his first senior game against Liverpool at Anfield in the second-to-last game of the season.

Abraham was in action again four days later, when he came on against Leicester City for his home debut and he was joined on the pitch by defender Fikayo Tomori, who got off the bench to make it three Academy-produced debutants in 2015/16.

On top of that, Charlie Colkett, Ola Aina and Kasey Palmer were all named as substitutes for first-team games during the 2015/16 campaign, showing that there is strength in depth coming through the ranks at Chelsea.

CHELSEA ACADEMY GRADUATES 2015/16

JAKE CLARKE-SALTER

Date of birth: 22.09.97
Place of birth: Carshalton
Position: Defender
First-team debut: 02.04.16 v Aston Villa
(Premier League)

TAMMY ABRAHAM

Date of birth: 02.10.97
Place of birth: Camberwell
Position: Striker
First-team debut: 11.05.16 v Liverpool
(Premier League)

FIKAYO TOMORI

Date of birth: 19.12.97
Place of birth: Calgary, Canada
Position: Defender
First-team debut: 15.05.16 v Leicester City
(Premier League)

OUR HEROES' HEROES

Every player had a favourite footballer when they were growing up, but who did they look up to outside the game?

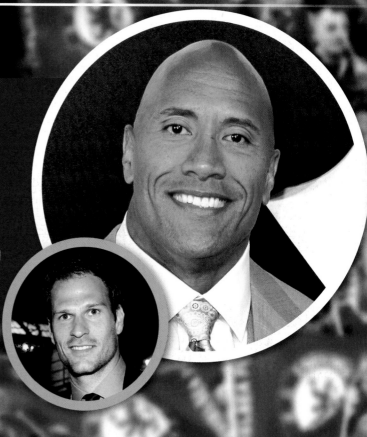

Dwayne 'The Rock' Johnson
Chosen by Asmir Begovic

I know it might sound cheesy to some but 'The Rock' really built up his career from nothing and I really like him. There is a story about him that he only had $7 in his pocket at one point and he was eating raw potatoes, but he has built himself up to become this multi-talented guy at a high level in many areas, so he is someone that I definitely look up to.

Jean-Claude Van Damme
Chosen by Kurt Zouma

When I was born, my father took the name of a Van Damme character in the film, *Kickboxer*, and gave it to me. That is why I am called Kurt. I like him – he is a crazy guy but he is also very funny.

Will Smith
Chosen by Ruben Loftus-Cheek

I like watching Will Smith movies, he is wicked in so many different things. He can do comedy or serious roles, he's got songs out, he's just one of those people that inspire you. He always comes out with quotes about being successful as well, which I admire.

Rafael Nadal
Chosen by Pedro

For me, he is an example for people in Spain, not just because of what he has achieved in his tennis career but also because of his attitude, his mentality. He is a great player in his sport and, for me, he is somebody to look up to.

Kriss Akabusi
Chosen by Gary Cahill

I used to really enjoy watching athletics as a kid and there were some really strong British athletes at the time. It's hard to pick out one person but the first name that comes to mind is Kriss Akabusi, the 400m hurdler – he had a lot of personality and the success to back it up.

Justine Henin and Kim Clijsters
Chosen by Eden Hazard

The tennis women! Both of them come from Belgium, like me, and they were among the best tennis players when they were still playing the game, winning a lot of important trophies. I don't play tennis very well, but I try. I play table-tennis more.

MEMBERSHIP 2016/17

Once a Blue, Always a Blue

ALL JUNIOR MEMBERSHIP PACKS INCLUDE
PRIORITY TICKET ACCESS AND AN EXCLUSIVE MEMBERSHIP PACK

FROM £20

ONCEABLUEALWAYSABLUE.COM

WHOSE BOOTS ARE THESE?

The boot room at Cobham has never been more colourful, but can you match these six players with the correct football boots?

GARY CAHILL   DIEGO COSTA
EDEN HAZARD   N'GOLO KANTÉ
CESC FÀBREGAS   RUBEN LOFTUS-CHEEK

You can find the answers on page 61.

STAMFORD LAUGHS

With a bit more practice Asmir will be ready to try driving with a real car.

Come on Diego, training's over.

No, I don't want to go home yet!

Cesc and Azpi never miss a chance to practice before the team karaoke night.

Mikel takes man-marking very seriously!

Pick it up lads, you're all over the place and it's only three days until the dance competition!

CHELSEA LADIES

Chelsea Ladies are one of the leading sides in the FA Women's Super League. As well as winning the Women's FA Cup in the first final held at Wembley Stadium, the Blues were also crowned league champions in 2015 and competed in the Champions League for the first time. Here's everything you need to know about Emma Hayes' squad...

FA WOMEN'S SUPER LEAGUE WINNERS 2015

The title race went right down to the wire, but Chelsea Ladies held their nerve to beat Sunderland 4-0 on the final day to win the championship for the first time in the club's history. Having scored the most goals and conceded the fewest, as well as leading from start to finish, the Blues were deserving winners.

PFA NOMINEES

Three Chelsea Ladies players were named in the PFA WSL Team of the Year: Niamh Fahey, Hedvig Lindahl and Ji So-Yun. The latter duo, along with Gemma Davison, were also on the shortlist to be crowned Women's Player of the Year – a prize Ji took home last year – while Hannah Blundell was in the running for the Young Player of the Year award. Here's how Emma Hayes rated each of the nominees.

JI-SO YUN

"Ji delivers the big goals in the big moments. When the team requires that, she delivers."

GEMMA DAVISON

"She is always trying to improve her technique in order to be the best she can be in one-on-one situations. In my opinion she is the best at that in Europe on her day."

HEDVIG LINDAHL

"She has that eccentricity that the best goalkeepers have and I appreciate it more and more with each passing year because I've realised what a special character it takes to be a goalkeeper."

HANNAH BLUNDELL

"Hannah will go on to become an England full-back, of that I have no doubt. She's got everything. She's improved so much defensively and she glides down the wing when she is attacking."

NEED TO KNOW:

Eniola Aluko was part of ITV's punditry team for the European Championship in France. In 2014 the Blues striker became the first female pundit in the 50-year history of the BBC's Match of the Day.

Manager Emma Hayes was awarded an MBE for services to football in the Queen's 90th Birthday Honours. However, she has yet to live up to her older sister's expectations. "She always said the most impressive thing I could do in life would be to go on a Question of Sport," joked the manager.

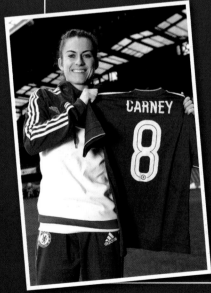

Striker Fran Kirby scored Chelsea's first-ever goal in the UEFA Women's Champions League when she smashed home an absolute worldie against Glasgow City in our debut in the competition.

Don't be surprised when you see Karen Carney jink her way past defenders for fun. The Blues midfielder, who has over 100 caps for England, used to be a champion disco dancer when she was younger!

Chelsea Ladies play their home games at Wheatsheaf Park, which is in Staines-upon-Thames. Tickets cost £3 for kids and £5 for adults. You can find more information on chelseafc.com.

Keep up to date with the Chelsea Ladies via their Twitter page, @ChelseaLFC.

THE KING OF STAMFORD BRIDGE

If you've ever been to watch Chelsea play at Stamford Bridge, there's a good chance you'll have seen a statue of Peter Osgood outside the West Stand. "Ossie", as he was known, was one of the greatest players ever to pull on a Blues shirt and he is the only man who has ever had a statue at the ground – that's how good he was!

Ossie played for Chelsea from 1964 to 1974, and again in the late Seventies. He scored an amazing 150 goals in 380 games, and in the 1969/70 season he netted in every round of the FA Cup to help Chelsea win the trophy for the first time. Ask older relatives about him and they will all say he was one of the best players they've ever seen. That's why they called him the King of Stamford Bridge.

Chelsea fans still adore Osgood. This picture was taken at the Stoke game in 2016, 10 years after he died.

This is Osgood at the age of 19, two years after he made his Chelsea debut when he scored two goals. A star was born.

Osgood scored an unbelievable diving header in the 1970 FA Cup final replay against Leeds United, which the Blues won 2-1 at Old Trafford. The first match at Wembley finished 2-2 and in those days, cup matches went to replays if they ended in a draw, rather than being decided on a penalty shoot-out.

E SHED CAME A RISING YOUNG STAR TLEY'S

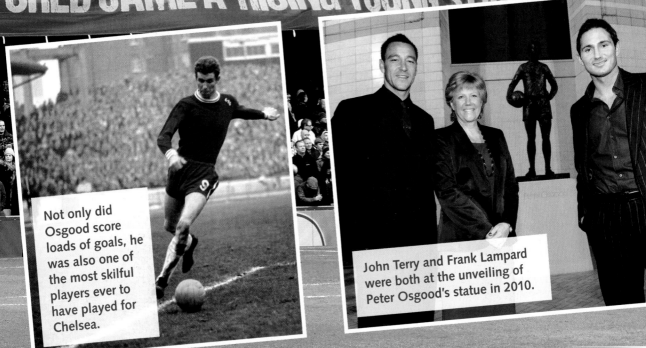

Not only did Osgood score loads of goals, he was also one of the most skilful players ever to have played for Chelsea.

John Terry and Frank Lampard were both at the unveiling of Peter Osgood's statue in 2010.

GUESS THE GOALSCORER

A club record 19 different players scored for Chelsea in the 2015/16 Premier League season, but can you identify each of our goalscorers with their faces covered up?

1 This Brazilian scored our first goal of the season against Swansea City.

2 3 4 Three Spanish players opened their account in our win at West Brom.

5 This player once scored a hat-trick against Chelsea for Atletico Madrid.

7 Keeping the opposition out is usually the aim of the game for this French centre-back.

6 A wonder strike from this midfielder couldn't earn us a victory at Everton.

8 9 A double dose of Brazilian magic earned us a draw at Newcastle.

10 World-class goals are nothing new for this centre-back.

The Blues slipped to defeat against the champions despite this goal by our No18.

A bullet header is nothing out of the ordinary for this Serbian defender.

This strike was simply fab-ulous!

No defender has scored more Premier League goals than this Blues hero.

With this goal he became the first player from Burkina Faso to score in the Premier League.

It took this Brazilian only 39 seconds to open the scoring against Norwich.

Hopefully the first Premier League goal of many for this Academy graduate.

Another Brazilian scorer for the Blues, who came off the bench to net on his debut against Villa.

After scoring against Bournemouth, this tricky little Belgian went on to net our Goal of the Season.

Answers on page 61

SOCCER SCHOOLS

BOYS AND GIRLS OF ALL ABILITIES AGED 4-13 YEARS

COURSES INCLUDE: MINI KICKERS, ADVANCED & GOALKEEPERS

Operating in the following areas:

Surrey, Berkshire, Middlesex, London, Essex, Hampshire, Wiltshire, Sussex & Kent

Visit chelseafc.com/foundation for your nearest venue

TIME TRAVELLER

Just for fun, let's see how five Blues stars would have looked if they'd played in a Chelsea team of the past...

A player of Cesc Fàbregas' talent would surely have been a star in any era of football, even in the tiny shorts of the late Seventies!

Goalkeepers like Thibaut Courtois had to get by without gloves in the Sixties.

A classic Chelsea kit for a classy player, as Eden Hazard heads back to the Eighties.

An old school centre-forward like Diego Costa would probably have fitted in pretty well in the early Nineties.

We're not sure if proud Italians like our head coach Antonio Conte and assistant Carlo Cudicini would have been keen on the "fashionable" suits of the Eighties.

BLUES AT THE EUROS

Several Chelsea players took part in the 2016 European Championship, when our new first-team head coach attracted his fair share of the limelight during the tournament.

Eden Hazard and Thibaut Courtois helped Belgium reach the quarter-finals and, before joining Chelsea, Antonio Conte led an unfancied Italy side to the same stage, when they were taken to penalties by Germany.

As usual, it was the Germans who came out on top in the shoot-out, but Blues fans got a glimpse of what they can expect from our new manager, who certainly shows plenty of passion on the touchline during games.

Here are some great pictures from the tournament involving the men in blue.

Getting the message across to his players

Antonio Conte celebrates Italy's win over Spain in the round of 16

Eden Hazard takes on the Wales defence in the quarter-finals

Celebrating his wonder goal against Hungary

Thibaut Courtois keeps the Republic of Ireland out

Punching the ball clear against Italy

Cesc Fàbregas celebrates after setting up a goal for Spain against Croatia

PLAYER OF THE YEAR

Willian became the 50th winner of Chelsea's Player of the Year award at the end of season dinner, but there were plenty of other prizes up for grabs on a memorable night at the Bridge.

GOAL OF THE SEASON: EDEN HAZARD v TOTTENHAM HOTSPUR

The Belgian winger became the second player to win this award for scoring a wonder goal against Tottenham Hotspur. His brilliant effort was selected as the best of the bunch from a choice of seven strikes. As well as being a beautiful goal, Hazard's strike meant we drew against Spurs, a result which ended their hopes of winning the title!

PLAYER OF THE YEAR & PLAYERS' PLAYER OF THE YEAR: WILLIAN

Only two players had previously won the Players' Player of the Year and the overall POTY prize on the same night: Juan Mata in 2013 and Eden Hazard last season. Willian can now be added to that list after a brilliant campaign in which his sensational free-kicks and endless running marked him out as the star man of the season.

YOUNG PLAYER OF THE YEAR: RUBEN LOFTUS-CHEEK

The Young Player of the Year is open to first-teamers under the age of 21, with the prize going to Ruben Loftus-Cheek on this occasion after he scored twice in 16 appearances in his first full campaign with the senior squad. He also starred for England's youngsters at the Toulon Tournament in the summer and was chosen as the best player at the event.

ACADEMY PLAYER OF THE YEAR: FIKAYO TOMORI

The Canadian-born defender enjoyed an incredible end to the 2015/16 season. He followed up this award, which was presented to him by Paulo Ferreira, by making his first-team debut on the final day of the season against Leicester City. Before that he had played in our UEFA Youth League and Youth Cup triumphs, scoring vital goals in both.

LADIES PLAYER OF THE YEAR: KATIE CHAPMAN

The Chelsea Ladies skipper succeeds Eniola Aluko as the club's Player of the Year, becoming just the second winner of the award. Chappers became the first Blues player to captain the Ladies to major silverware as we won both the Women's FA Cup and Super League titles, and she also played a big part in England's World Cup campaign.

COMPETITION

WIN A SIGNED CHELSEA SHIRT!

Answer the following question correctly and you could win a Chelsea shirt signed by a first-team player!

> What is the name of the song released by Chelsea FC and Suggs when we reached the FA Cup final in 1997?

A) Blue Moon   B) Blue Monday   C) Blue Day

Entry is by email only. Only one entry per contestant. Please enter CFC SHIRT followed by either A, B, or C in the subject line of an email. In the body of the email, please include your full name, address, postcode, email address, phone number and date of birth and send to:

frontdesk@grangecommunications.co.uk by Friday 31st March 2017.

Ben from Surrey was delighted to win last year's signed shirt competition.

Competition Terms and Conditions

1) The closing date for this competition is Friday 31st March 2017 at midnight. Entries received after that time will not be counted.

2) Information on how to enter and on the prize form part of these conditions.

3) Entry is open to those residing in the UK only. If entrants are under 18, consent from a parent or guardian must be obtained and the parent or guardian must agree to these terms and conditions. If entrants are under 13, this consent must be given in writing from the parent or guardian with their full contact details.

4) This competition is not open to employees or their relatives of Chelsea Football Club. Any such entries will be invalid.

5) The start date for entries is 31st October 2016 at 4pm.

6) Entries must be strictly in accordance with these terms and conditions. Any entry not in strict accordance with these terms and conditions will be deemed to be invalid and no prize will be awarded in respect of such entry. By entering, all entrants will be deemed to accept these rules.

7) One (1) lucky winner will win a 2016/17 season signed football shirt.

8) The prize is non-transferable and no cash alternative will be offered. Entry is by email only. Only one entry per contestant. Please enter CFC SHIRT followed by either A, B or C in the subject line of an email. In the body of the email, please include your full name, address, postcode, email address and phone number and send to: frontdesk@grangecommunications.co.uk by Friday 31st March 2017.

9) The winner will be picked at random. The winner will be contacted within 72 hours of the closing date. Details of the winner can be requested after this time from the address below.

10) Entries must not be sent in through agents or third parties. No responsibility can be accepted for lost, delayed, incomplete, or for electronic entries or winning notifications that are not received or delivered. Any such entries will be deemed void.

11) The winner will have 72 hours to claim their prize once initial contact has been made by the Promoter. Failure to respond may result in forfeiture of the prize.

12) At Chelsea FC plc and our group companies, we go the extra mile to ensure that your personal information is kept secure and safe. We will not release it to outside companies to use but we'd like your permission to keep in touch and tell you about relevant news, offers and promotions from ourselves and on behalf of our official sponsors and partners. If you would prefer not to receive these messages you can opt out by emailing CFC STOP to frontdesk@grangecommunications. co.uk before midnight on Friday 31st March 2017. Your information will always be safeguarded under the terms and conditions of the Data Protection Act 1998 and CFC's Privacy Policy (http://www.chelseafc. com/the-club/legal/privacy-policy.html) to ensure that the information you provide is safe.

13) The Promoter reserves the right to withdraw or amend the promotion as necessary due to circumstances outside its reasonable control. The Promoter's decision on all matters is final and no correspondence will be entered into.

14) The Promoter (or any third party nominated by the Promoter) may use the winner's name and image and their comments relating to the prize for future promotional, marketing and publicity purposes in any media worldwide without notice and without any fee being paid.

15) Chelsea Football Club's decision is final; no correspondence will be entered in to. Except in respect of death or personal injury resulting from any negligence of the Club, neither Chelsea Football Club nor any of its officers, employees or agents shall be responsible for (whether in tort, contract or otherwise):

(i) any loss, damage or injury to you and/or any guest or to any property belonging to you or any guest in connection with this competition and/ or the prize, resulting from any cause whatsoever;

(ii) for any loss of profit, loss of use, loss of opportunity or any indirect, economic or consequential losses whatsoever.

16) This competition shall be governed by English law.

17) Promoter: Grange Communications Ltd, 22 Great King Street, Edinburgh EH3 6QH.

2016/17 KITS

Once again, Chelsea and adidas have combined for a stylish set of kits for the 2016/17 season.

The home shirt, which made its debut at Wembley Stadium when the Chelsea Ladies wore it in the FA Women's Cup final, and the third kit are both classic blue and white strips, keeping Chelsea's traditions going strong into 2017.

The away kit and training gear – the second featuring the logo of our new partner Carabao for the first time – go for an eye-catching look, with the grey, black and neon-yellow combination sure to stand out on the pitch at Stamford Bridge and Cobham.

If you want to look the part and match the style of the Blues stars, you can get all our 2016/17 kits from the Stamford Bridge Megastore, Chelsea Store in Kingston or online at www.chelseafc.com/shopping.

ANSWERS

P24 BLUES AROUND THE WORLD

1g. Spain (Cesc Fàbregas)

2d. Portugal (Eduardo)

3f. Belgium (Eden Hazard)

4b. Brazil (Willian)

5e. France (N'Golo Kanté)

6h. Nigeria (John Mikel Obi)

7a. Italy (Antonio Conte)

8c. England (Gary Cahill)

P43 WHOSE BOOTS ARE THESE?

Cesc Fàbregas

Diego Costa

Eden Hazard

Ruben Loftus-Cheek

N'Golo Kanté

Gary Cahill

P27 GUESS WHO?

WILLIAN

HAZARD

KANTÉ

IVANOVIC

P50 GUESS THE GOALSCORER

1 – Oscar
2 – Diego Costa
3 – Pedro
4 – Cesar Azpilicueta
5 – Radamel Falcao
6 – Nemanja Matic
7 – Kurt Zouma
8 – Ramires
9 – Willian
10 – Gary Cahill
11 – Loic Remy
12 – Branislav Ivanovic
13 – Cesc Fàbregas
14 – John Terry
15 – Bertrand Traore
16 – Kenedy
17 – Ruben Loftus-Cheek
18 – Alexandre Pato
19 – Eden Hazard

WHERE'S STAMFORD?

Stamford the Lion is hiding somewhere in the crowd at Stamford Bridge, but can you find him?